The Happy Place

A Children's Book of Spiritual Values Concerning Issues Faced When Becoming Adolescents

CHERI BETH ROSHON

BALBOA.
PRESS
A DIVISION OF HAY HOUSE

Balboa Press books may be ordered through booksellers or by contacting:

Balboa Press
A Division of Hay House
1663 Liberty Drive
Bloomington, IN 47403
www.balboapress.com
1 (877) 407-4847

Because of the dynamic nature of the Internet, any web addresses or links contained in this book may have changed since publication and may no longer be valid. The views expressed in this work are solely those of the author and do not necessarily reflect the views of the publisher, and the publisher hereby disclaims any responsibility for them.

The author of this book does not dispense medical advice or prescribe the use of any technique as a form of treatment for physical, emotional, or medical problems without the advice of a physician, either directly or indirectly. The intent of the author is only to offer information of a general nature to help you in your quest for emotional and spiritual well-being. In the event you use any of the information in this book for yourself, which is your constitutional right, the author and the publisher assume no responsibility for your actions.

Any people depicted in stock imagery provided by Thinkstock are models, and such images are being used for illustrative purposes only.
Certain stock imagery © Thinkstock.

Print information available on the last page.

ISBN: 978-1-5043-7855-0 (sc)
ISBN: 978-1-5043-7857-4 (hc)
ISBN: 978-1-5043-7856-7 (e)

Library of Congress Control Number: 2017905678

Balboa Press rev. date: 04/28/2017

Dedication

A children's book of spiritual values concerning issues faced when becoming adolescents. Lesson segments follow each chapter.

The longer we wait to tie into a new concious awareness, a Universal Source, the greater becomes the distance between the warmth of the original God connection and the coldness of solitary human existence. This is where we lose ourselves, and our children. If only we can show our children this spiritual connection early in life, hopefully the confusion of purpose in adolescence can be avoided. It is to them, our children, that I dedicate this book. With Love, Cheri Beth Roshon

ACKNOWLEDGEMENTS

I would like to express my appreciation to a few of the many people who made this book possible.

First and foremost, I want to thank my 4 daughters who inspired me to not only live my dream, but also encouraged my desire to write a book that could help children as they grow through the tough times toward adulthood. My hope is that my grandchildren will have a fun guideline to avert the stresses of everyday living.

Secondly, I wish to thank Audrey Wyman for seeing I had a dream and contributing the first monies to print my manuscript so I could send it to prospective publishers. Audrey is no longer with us here on Earth, but a part of her will live on through this book, because she believed in me.

Next my appreciation goes out to Dr. C. Norman Shealy for his inspirational work and for his kindness in reading The Happy Place. His encouragement and well wishes along the way kept me going, and for that, I am eternally grateful.

On to my friend "Loon" who not only proofed the completed manuscript and kept me inspired, but also found the perfect artist, Solange Brown, for the cover of my book, and for bringing Divinity to life. All this inspiration made it impossible to procrastinate any longer!

And last but never least to you, my dear readers, for taking the time to pick up this book and take a chance that something in it will inspire you to help others rather than walk away from any difficulties you may face.

With Love, Cheri Beth Roshon

CONTENTS

CHAPTER 1

One Summer Adventure

Molly and Brin were the best of friends. They had lived next door to each other since they were very young. Theirs was a small town where every person knew every other person, and it was a good place to grow up.

School was out for the summer, and Molly and Brin decided to do something special for summer vacation. Being out of school was nice, but they wanted to make this a summer to remember.

On Monday morning, Brin came over to Molly's house and asked her if she wanted to go exploring. That sounded like fun, so Molly asked her mother if it would be okay. Her mother thought that was a good idea, so off they went. On the walk, they saw a lot of kids throwing balls back and forth, and playing hopscotch on the sidewalk, but they didn't even stop to say hello. They wanted to get to the edge of town where the woods began. Brin had an idea. He knew of a path that led to a pond in a small clearing in the woods, not too far from town. "Come on Molly, I'll show you how to get to the pond today!" said Brin

"That sounds like fun," replied Molly. She was thinking maybe there was something special at the pond.

Along the path they passed some wondrous sights. A mother bird was feeding her hungry babies in a nest up in a big old tree. Two squirrels were playing tag from treetop to treetop. Brin thought he could almost hear them laughing together! Molly found some spring violets tucked away under some new green leaves, still fresh with dew. "Oh, Brin," cried Molly, "There are such beautiful things here in the woods. This must be a very special place!"

"Yes," answered Brin, "and I can hardly wait to get to the pond!"

On they walked, watching for any new sights and sounds. Brin found a green caterpillar on a tree twig, and put it in his hand. "Look, Molly, this caterpillar is a special thing. Remember what Mrs. Herman taught us in our science class last year?"

Molly thought for a moment, and said "Oh yes, I remember! This plain old caterpillar just spends its days eating leaves and crawling around in search of more leaves. One day he will spin a cocoon, and after working hard to get it just right, he will go to sleep in it. When he wakes up, he will burst through the cocoon as a beautiful butterfly!"

Brin thoughtfully placed the caterpillar back where he had found it, thinking of all the hard work the caterpillar had ahead of it to bring about the changes that would make him a beautiful butterfly, with wings and everything.

The closer they got to the pond, the more noises they heard. "Let's stop and listen, Molly", said Brin. "Do you know what those noises are?"

Molly and Brin sat down on a fallen log, and listened. There was the sound of splashing frogs, hopping from Lilly pad to Lilly pad.

There were catbirds calling to each other in the trees. The crickets were rubbing their back legs together, making pond music. Some of the noises Molly didn't know, but it all sounded so peaceful. "Let's go to the pond, Brin! I want to see it for myself!"

So they walked further down the path, and sure enough, around the next turn, was a clearing in the woods, with a pond right in the middle of it! "Oh, Brin! This IS a special place!" cried Molly. "I am so glad we came looking for it!"

"I have an idea, Molly. This can be our special place for the summer. We can build a clubhouse out of old boxes and stuff, and have a real neat secret place!"

"Oh, yes!" agreed Molly as she clapped her hands with delight. "And we will be the only ones who know about it! This will be the BEST summer adventure!"

CHAPTER 1 LESSONS

Know---We know there is more in our world than we can see with our eyes. There are things bigger than what we can see everyday in our mundane world. Knowing this is the first step.

Seek and Find---When we KNOW there is more, we need only to look for it with the belief that we WILL find it, and we will succeed.

Pay attention---When we find the "more" that we seek, we must pay attention to it to discover the mysteries in it. By paying attention to it, we give it energy and discover more about it.

Focus---When we then focus on it with intent, we see beyond what we thought we saw. Just like the caterpillar who spends all day eating leaves, we as humans spend our lives gathering experiences. As we integrate these experiences into our lives, it is as if wrapping ourselves in a cocoon, digesting what we learn when we focus. All the lessons bring us to a new understanding.

Transformation---With the new understanding, we transform ourselves into a new being, breaking the shell of our self-imposed cocoon, and coming into the Light, as a butterfly with wings.

Meditation---In our new awareness, we hear with new ears, and see with new eyes. If we but stop the busyness and listen, we will find the next step.

CHAPTER 2

The Clubhouse

Early the next day, Molly and Brin were ready for their new adventure. They had agreed on the way home from the woods to tell only their parents about the new place. Not only would letting their parents know where they were be the safe thing to do, but they also knew they would need help getting just the right materials to build the new clubhouse.

Brin came over to Molly's house right after breakfast with some old scraps of wood, and a blanket in his wagon. Molly met him at the door with her dad's old hammer and some shiny new nails. "Hi Brin, are you ready to go?" asked Molly.

"Yes, I am, Molly! Just look at all this wood Grandpa Johanson let us have!"

"Great! Oh, what's the blanket for?" Molly wondered out loud.

"It's our DOOR, Molly. We need a door for our secret meetings---you know--JUST IN CASE." replied Brin secretively.

"Oooohhhh" said Molly slowly. She may not know much about door building, but she knew Brin, and she could tell he had a plan. "Mom, we're leaving" called Molly.

"Wait a minute, you two." said Molly's mother as she came to the front door. "Such hard working children will get hungry and need to take a lunch break. Here are some sandwiches and juice and cookies for you."

"Thanks, Mom," smiled Molly as she kissed her mother goodbye.

"Yeah, thanks Mrs. Bennett," called Brin as he headed toward the woods.

Molly and Brin found their way through the woods right to their special place in no time. They were very excited, and wanted to get started on the new clubhouse. "Well, here we are," said Brin. "Where shall we start?"

Brin was the kind of boy who wanted to jump right in and get things done. But he knew Molly liked to plan things out and do a good job, so he waited for her answer. "Hmmmm, remember when my dad built a doghouse for Sparky, Brin?"

Brin nodded yes, and Molly continued. "He had plans, and knew how big he wanted the doghouse. He knew just how long to cut the wood pieces, and he measured it all out. I thought we might need a plan, so I drew my ideas on paper last night."

"Good idea, Molly, let me see it." Brin looked over Molly's plan, and they talked about how big it should be, and where they would put it. After a long discussion, they were both happy with their plan. "Let's eat now," said Brin, "and then we'll get to work."

"Okay," laughed Molly, and that's just what they did.

Later that day, there was an almost finished clubhouse in the special place in the woods. Molly and Brin were happy but tired after working all day. "Let's go home, Molly," said Brin. "I'll come by and get you tomorrow morning."

So the hard working children walked slowly through the woods, not talking much. They were both dreaming of their new clubhouse and all the fun they would have that summer. "Say, Brin," said Molly slowly, "we should name our new clubhouse, don't you think?"

"Yes, Molly," answered Brin. "I think we should call it The Happy Place."

CHAPTER 2 LESSONS

Align Intentions----When an idea comes to you, thought of which direction is the best follows. Being sure that the order is set makes the process easier.

Ask questions, define answers---You must ask the right questions to find the answers you seek. Giving time to the process uncovers answers you may not previously have thought of.

Gratitude---Every time something in your life becomes clear, give thanks for the answer.

Once you know----When the answers are clear, so is the proper way of commencing.

Cooperation and listening to others---Getting new perspectives enhances knowledge and adds pieces you may not have thought of.

Purpose---Once you have aligned all the possibilities and chosen the proper way, it becomes clear what you must do.

Do it---Get started with an open mind. Be open to all possibilities without control.

Contemplation---Now take your time, review the progress, and make changes as necessary.

CHAPTER 3

The Fun Begins

True to his word, Brin was at Molly's house the next day. They went straight to work, finishing their clubhouse. They realized that the finished product would take time, and many things could be done to make it truly special. They left an open place for the door, and hung the blanket over it. They had a window, and Mrs. Bennett had given them a piece of pretty material for a curtain. Molly thought they should paint it, too, so she asked Brin what he thought.

"Well, Molly, we would have to find some paint first, and agree on the color," said Brin. He was thinking she might want to paint it pink, or something he wouldn't like. After all, it should be something cool, and not girly. They decided white would be a good color, and easy to find. The next few days were spent putting the finishing touches on the clubhouse, and they knew they would have the best clubhouse ever. What they didn't know was that someone was watching them!

On Thursday, when Molly and Brin were walking through the woods and laughing about how much fun they were having, Billy, the new boy in town, was sitting up in a tree. He had heard the laughter, and looked down to see Molly and Brin carrying a lunchbox and some paint, and heading into the woods. "Now what do you suppose they're up to?" thought Billy. So he quietly climbed down from the tree and followed the kids. When they got to the clearing by the pond, Billy hid behind a bush and watched. Molly and Brin were having so much fun! This was no fair! He wanted to have a cool clubhouse, too! He sneaked back to town to think about what to do.

Finished at last, Molly and Brin sat down to admire their work. The sun was shining brightly, so they closed their eyes and were very proud of themselves, thinking about all the work they'd done to create this fine clubhouse. "I feel so happy, Brin! We have done a great job!" said Molly, still with her eyes shut.

"Happiness is created when a goal is reached," said a voice from out of nowhere.

"What?" asked Molly.

"What?" asked Brin.

"What did you say, Molly?" asked Brin again.

Molly looked at Brin with wide eyes. "I didn't say anything Brin---I thought it was YOU!"

"Happiness is created when a goal is reached." came the voice again.

"Who said that?" cried Brin, jumping to his feet.

Molly jumped up, too, and held on to Brin's arm. "Yeah! Who said that?" she echoed.

"Look inside, for I am here." said the voice.

Looking instead at each other with questioning eyes, Molly and Brin were unable to move for a moment, but the voice said, "Do not be afraid. You asked for an adventure, did you not? Come inside and you will see."

Slowly, holding hands, Molly and Brin went through the blanket-door, and stepped inside. There they saw the most spectacular thing they had ever seen! A small fairylike being was fluttering around inside their clubhouse! They both gasped in surprise! "Brin, it's a butterfly!" exclaimed Molly.

Brin was just staring, no words coming out of his mouth. "Brin, DO something!" Molly almost yelled. Now Brin was very protective of Molly, because she was his best friend. He grabbed a small stick and held it high. But the little being laughed, and her laughter sounded like bells or chimes, and Brin was so surprised, he dropped the stick. "Who are you?" he asked in his bravest voice.

"You can call me Divinity." said the fairy-like being.

"What are you doing in our clubhouse?" asked Brin, still trying to be brave.

"Well, you asked for a special adventure, did you not?"

"Yes." said Molly and Brin together.

"Well, you asked, and here I am!"

Well, Molly and Brin didn't know what to say, so they just stared at Divinity. She was so beautiful, and she seemed so nice that the children were no longer afraid. "I am here to help you," said Divinity. "There are many things I can teach you, if you are willing to learn."

"Okay," replied Molly, "but WHAT are you, and where did you come from?"

"I am your inner Light, your imagination, and your friend, all in one." said Divinity. "I know of the ways of life, and I can help you to be better people, if you will but listen, and learn." As Molly and Brin were too stunned to respond, Divinity went on. "I am your inner knowing that will help you when you are scared, angry or confused. Everyone has a special friend like me, if only they wish to see. I can show you a better way of seeing any situation, because I am a part of Love."

Well, Molly and Brin didn't know what to say! Finally Brin asked a question. "Why did you come to our clubhouse, Divinity?"

Divinity smiled and laughed her musical laugh. "I wanted you to see that when you set out to DO something, and you work together and cooperate, the job is well done, and you should feel proud. You asked for a special summer, and so that is what you shall have, if you still want it!"

"Oh yes!" the children replied together. "So what do we do next?" asked Molly.

"Well, let's get to know each other," said Divinity, and so they did.

CHAPTER 3 LESSONS

Follow Through---When you have an idea and it feels right, follow it to the end, and experience the results.

Cooperate---Working together gives you new ideas and builds upon the basic idea.

Blocks---Sometimes when we are in the process of creating our goal, we find unexpected blocks that we have to deal with.

Happiness is created when your goal is achieved---You can have pride in what you accomplish.

Look inside yourself (heart)---When you close your eyes and look into your heart center, you find the spark of God (Divinity).

Unexpected results---When you ask for something to happen and it does, (ask and you shall receive), sometimes you get more than what you hoped for, or in a different way.

Ask and receive---Seek and you shall find. When you ask for something and it is for your highest good, you will receive it.

Be open---When you remove obstacles and have an open mind, you will see things you never knew existed.

Guide---We all have an inner knowing to guide us through our life.

CHAPTER 4

The Bully

Meanwhile, Billy had gone home to think about those kids and that clubhouse they had built. "Why should THEY have a cool clubhouse like that?" thought Billy. "I don't have a clubhouse like that, so THEY shouldn't have one, either!" Just thinking about how much fun those kids were having started to make Billy mad. He got so mad, he decided that he would go back to the pond and wreck that ol' clubhouse so Molly and Brin would be mad too, and so they couldn't have fun anymore!

As he tried to remember how to get to the clearing in the woods, he got frustrated. "I can't remember where that darn clubhouse is!" he cried in anger. But Billy was a very smart boy, and he remembered how he got to the tree where he saw Molly and Brin, so he went there first. He climbed up into the tree, and thought hard about which direction they had gone. He climbed down the tree, and went the way he thought was right. Sure enough, soon he could hear laughter coming from the clearing in the woods, so he hid behind the same bush as before, and waited. The longer he waited and listened to the kids having fun, the madder he got. All he could think about was that it was so unfair that those kids were having fun, and he was not.

By and by, Molly and Brin came out of the clubhouse laughing, and started on their way home. Billy waited until he could no longer hear their voices, and went toward the clubhouse, wanting to destroy it completely! He looked around to see how he could tear it apart, and grabbed onto the wooden walls, but they were very solid. Molly and Brin had indeed done a great job! He looked around for a better way to wreck it.......

In the meantime, Molly and Brin were partway home when they remembered they had forgotten their lunch pails at the clubhouse. They were so amazed that they had met Divinity, they'd completely forgotten to bring their stuff home! They turned around and went back to the pond. When they arrived, what did they see but a boy trying to tear down their blanket they had hung up for a door! He was yelling and tugging at the door, and it ripped in half! Brin was so mad he yelled "Stop it!" and raced for the other boy. He was ready to punch Billy right in the nose, when Divinity appeared out of nowhere and said, "No Brin. Stop and think first," in her gentle and loving voice. Brin stopped just before his fist hit Billy's nose because he didn't expect Divinity to be there. "Why should I stop? This boy is wrecking our clubhouse!" yelled Brin.

Now, Billy couldn't see who or what Brin was talking to, so he was not only surprised at the children's return, but he was expecting a bloody nose, and all of a suddden this strange boy started talking to…NOBODY! "What's going on?" cried Billy, and realizing he had a chance to get away, he ran as fast as he could into the woods!

Molly and Brin could see Divinity now, because they had accepted her into their lives. Divinity said, "All is not as it seems," and disappeared into the clubhouse. Molly and Brin followed her in, and sat down.

"Why didn't you let me hit that kid?" asked Brin, still angry that someone had not only found their clubhouse, but was trying to destroy it. "He will just come back and try it again! What can we do?"

Divinity replied, "Since you ask, I will tell you. Go find that boy. Ask him to join your club."

"WHAT?" yelled Molly and Brin at the same time. "We don't want a bully in our clubhouse!" sniffled Molly. "I hate him!"

"You don't know him, therefore how can you hate him?" asked Divinity calmly. "If you try hard, you can understand why he is the way he is. Do you want to try?"

"Okay," said both children slowly, although neither one was sure they wanted to try to understand at all. "We'll try," said Molly.

"This boy is jealous of your happiness. Sometimes when a person has no joy of their own, they resent anyone who is happy," explained Divinity.

"But why isn't he happy?" asked Brin. "And what can WE do about it?"

"Thank you for asking, Brin, because it shows you do care," replied Divinity. "This boy is new in town, and he has no friends. His dad lost his job, so they moved here, looking for work. His dad is very frustrated, and sometimes he gets so mad at himself, he hits Billy."

"Oh, how awful!" cried Molly. "Is that why he is so angry?"

"Yes, Molly," Divinity replied. "His father is mean to Billy, so Billy is learning to be a bully when he gets frustrated. And he has no friends to be happy with, so what do you suppose can be done about this?"

"Ohhhh, I see where you're going with this," said Brin. "You want US to find him, and be his friend!"

Divinity beamed and she said, "Yes! Go make yourself a new friend if you can find it in your heart to show Billy a better way!"

The kids weren't too sure about this, but they agreed to do their best, and went looking for Billy.

CHAPTER 4 LESSONS

Negative attention---When someone has something you want, and you can't have it, it can create bad feelings. If we dwell on what we DON"T have, we get frustrated. Instead we should look at what we DO have, and be happy. If we want more than what we have, then we should look for a way to accomplish that, and get what we want in a positive way. Negative actions bring more negative actions, but positive attracts positive actions and feelings.

Re-create---When we forget where we've been, we must re-create the situation in our mind, and see how we accomplished it before.

Judgement---We may never rightfully judge another human being or situation. We don't know why people are the way they are, and why they do what they do. All we can do is either accept people the way they are, or try our best to show them a better way to be, by setting a good example.

To be in another's place---When you understand WHY a person is the way he is, you can better understand why they react to life's situations the way they do.

CHAPTER 5

Forgiveness

The next day, Molly and Brin thought about looking for Billy. "Our town is pretty small," said Molly. "We should be able to find him."

"Yeah, Molly, but are we sure we WANT to find him? What if he doesn't want to be our friend?" asked Brin.

"Well, I think we should give him a chance, Brin. Isn't that what we would want someone to do for us?" In the silence that followed Molly's question, the children heard Divinity's voice. She said, "Treat others as you would like to be treated." The children looked knowingly at each other, and the decision was made. They went to find Billy.

After asking many questions of the townspeople, they found out where Billy lived. It was a small house just outside of town. Getting their courage together, they went and found Billy's house, and knocked on the door. A large, mean looking man answered the door. "Yeah? What do you want?" he asked gruffly.

"Um, is Billy home?" gulped Brin, trying to look brave.

"Maybe!" said Billy's father. "What did he do to you?" and he glared at them menacingly.

"Nothing, Sir," replied Molly in her sweetest voice. "We just thought he might want to play."

The man looked at the children on his doorstep for a good hard minute, and turned inside and yelled, "Billy, get out here!"

Billy came to the door, and when he saw Molly and Brin, he started to say something, but his father said, "These kids want you to play. Get out of here!", so Billy came outside. As his father slammed the door, Billy tried to look tough, but before he could say anything, Brin said, "Hey Billy, do you want to join our club?"

Billy looked very surprised! He didn't know what to say, so Molly said, "Come on, Billy, we have something to show you," and off they went. On the way to the clubhouse, Molly tried to tell Billy why they came to his house. She did her best to explain. "You see, Billy, Brin and I thought that maybe, since you are new and all, you might be looking for some new friends, so we came to see you."

Again, Billy didn't know what to say. He stumbled on his words. "But, I mean, WHY would you want me to be your friend? I'm no good! I wanted to wreck your clubhouse….why are you being so nice to me?"

"Because we have a friend who understands you," said Billy. "Would you like to meet her?"

"But how would she know me?" asked Billy. "We just moved here."

"Well Billy, she is a very special friend, and she knows many things.

She is kind of…well, different…but if you can keep a secret, she would like you to see her." said Molly.

"A secret? Yes, I can keep a secret! Hey, this is kind of mysterious…. this is FUN!" said Billy. 'Let's hurry up and meet her!" And off they went!

CHAPTER 5 LESSONS

Vulnerability---Sometimes we are afraid if we open ourselves up to someone, they will hurt us. But being vulnerable is just another way of opening up to a new experience. If we never try, we will never know.

Do unto others----The Golden Rule. If we would all treat each other the way we want to be treated, the world would be a much better place. We would be thoughtful and kind to one another, and share what we have, so no one would go without.

Courage---It takes courage to face our fears. By facing them, we deal with them, and can know the outcome of our actions. Sometimes it may not be a good result, but at least we know we have done our best. Other times, we gain much from facing our fears, and dealing with them instead of hiding from them, only to forever wonder "what if?"

Sharing---If we can share the joy, or the knowledge we have found or been given with others, it multiplies our own joy in the mere act of giving to others that which we already have.

CHAPTER 6

Sharing Kindness

The kids got to the clubhouse in no time. When they were about to go through the door that Billy had torn in half, Billy stopped and hung his head. "Hey, you two, I just want to say I am sorry for wrecking your door. I don't know what made me do it, but I was just so....angry!"

"We know, Billy," said Molly kindly. "Divinity explained it to us."

"Who's Divinity? How does she know about me? I don't understand." Billy looked like he was going to cry, so Brin said quickly, "Let's go inside so you can meet her!"

"Here?" asked Billy, "But I......"

"Come on, Billy, let's just go inside!" said Molly.

Once they were inside the clubhouse, Molly told the boys to sit down. "I want to try to explain something, Billy, so you will understand. If you want to see her, just close your eyes, and tell her you're ready....c'mon, just try!" So Billy did what Molly said.

"Divinity, Billy is here, and he is really a nice boy. He is ready to see you now. Please join us," said Molly in a soft voice.

"Well, hello Billy." came a voice from somewhere over Billy's head.

Billy opened his eyes, and when he saw Divinity, he was so surprised, he jumped to his feet and started to say, "What the…." Divinity's laughter filled the clubhouse like the tinkling of bells.

"We TOLD you she was different!" laughed Brin.

Billy stood with his mouth wide open, just staring at the beautiful fairy being who was fluttering around the clubhouse.

"You see Billy, I am like the Light inside of you. You can see me now because you were brave enough to give Molly and Brin a chance to be your friends. Don't be afraid. I am here to help you understand things that confuse you. You can talk to me, and I can help you to see things in a different way. What do you wish to know?"

The kindness in Divinity's voice almost made Billy cry. "I'm no good" he choked. "Why would you want to help me?"

"You are a child of God, Billy, and you are a good person. What makes you think you are no good?" asked Divinity.

"My dad says so." sobbed Billy. "He hates me. Sometimes he hits me, and it hurts!"

By now, Billy was really crying. Molly put her arm around Billy's shoulder, and Divinity answered, "Your father doesn't hate you, Billy, he is frustrated with himself. Sometimes when people see no hope for themselves, they take it out on the ones they love."

"But it HURTS when he hits me." sniffled Billy, hanging his head in embarrassment.

"I know, Billy, and it doesn't just hurt in a physical way. It hurts your feelings, too, because you love your dad, and you want him to love you, too. The important thing for you to know is your dad DOES love you, and he wants to do his best to provide for you and your family. When that seems impossible, he loses hope, and sometimes turns to violence to let his anger out. It's not RIGHT to do that, but he feels like a failure, and he wants everyone around him to feel bad, too." explained Divinity in her gentle way.

"See, Billy, I TOLD you she knows things," said Brin. "She explained that to us the day I wanted to punch you in the nose!"

"Ohhhh," said Billy slowly. "I think I understand now. I think I get it! When my dad gets angry, he takes it out on me. That makes ME angry. Then, when I saw you two having fun, and I was NOT having fun, I wanted to wreck YOUR fun. And when Brin saw me wrecking HIS fun, he wanted to hurt ME!"

"Very good, Billy," said Divinity. "Anger brings more anger, and it spreads from one person to the next. Soon, everyone is angry, and the happiness is gone. What do you think we can do to solve this problem?"

"I don't know," replied Billy quietly. "I just don't know how to help my dad not to be angry."

"Well," Brin said slowly, "I know when I saw you trying to wreck our clubhouse, I wanted to punch you good. But Divinity stopped me. She told me that I needed to see things from your eyes, and she explained to me about your dad. Then she told us what you needed most was for us to understand why you were angry, and to show you we could be your friends. That made the difference, right Divinity?"

"Very good, Brin!" exclaimed Divinity. "So, what's the next step, children?"

"Well, we can start by understanding," said Molly.

'Yes! And I can tell my dad that I know he will find work soon, and show him I love him, even if he does get angry!" exclaimed Billy.

"Very good, Billy," Divinity beamed. "And I will tell you another thing you can do. Close your eyes and focus on your dad getting a job. See it clearly in your mind. All of you, together do this, and be sincere, and I promise you, it will come to be."

"Okay, Divinity, we will!" said all three children, and that's just what they did.

CHAPTER 6 LESSONS

Repentance---When we are truly sorry in our heart about things we have done, we change inside. We become humble, and do our best not to repeat the bad we've done.

Open to a different perspective---there are things all around us that we don't choose to see sometimes, because we don't even know they're there. Once we open our minds, different possibilities come to us, and we become more aware.

Melt barriers---When we understand the actions of another person, and we see things the way they do, our differences don't seem so big, and what has kept us separate, now binds us together.

Worthiness---Once we realize we are worthy of love, bad feelings can be replaced by good feelings.

Violence begets violence---Energy is transferred to others when we react to situations. If it is a negative situation, anger brings more anger. If it is joy, joy passes from one person to another. How we react is our CHOICE.

CHAPTER 7

The New Girl

Well, it took some time, but the children now knew they had a way to help Billy and his dad. Divinity had told them in the very beginning, "ask and you shall get what you ask for," and they believed her. Billy's dad did get a job, and since he wasn't so angry anymore, he started to treat Billy better. He even took Billy to a baseball game. He never did apologize for hitting his only son, but Billy knew why his dad had been so mean, so he felt much better about it, and he didn't need an apology.

So the days went by, and the kids went to the clubhouse whenever they could. They played in the woods, and swam in the pond, and soon it was like they had known Billy forever. They were great friends.

One day Molly overheard her mother talking to one of their neighbors. "Oh, isn't it awful about Beth?" Mrs. Bennett had said to her friend. "And the doctors don't know how long she has to live, poor thing!"

Molly asked her mother what she was talking about. "Well Honey, little Beth down the street is very ill, and the doctors don't know if she will make it."

"Oh no, Mom! What shall we do?" asked Molly.

"Best to leave the family alone, I think," replied Mrs. Bennett. "Yes, they probably need to be left alone."

Molly was very upset. She ran over to Brin's house where Billy and Brin were playing and said, "Come on guys, we need Divinity, and we need her NOW!"

"What's up, Molly?" asked Brin. He had never seen her this way before.

"Just let's go," said Molly, and off they went.

As they ran to the clubhouse, Molly told the boys what her mother had said. "We need to ask Divinity what to do to help!" cried Molly.

When they reached the clubhouse, they all sat down and closed their eyes. In their minds, they all called for Divinity to come. In the twinkling of an eye, Divinity appeared. "What is it, children? What do you need to know?"

Molly told her about Beth, and what her mother had said. "What can we do to help?" asked Molly with tears in her eyes.

"Well, I can see that your mother thinks that the family is upset, and needs to be left alone," said Divinity slowly. "Sometimes adults think that way. She is afraid if she goes to see Beth's family that they will think she is intruding. But what is really going on is your mother doesn't want to see a little girl suffering, because it makes it more real to her that it could happen to her family, too. Sometimes adults ignore things that they are afraid of."

"Is my mom a bad person because she doesn't want to help?" asked Molly with tears in her eyes.

"No, no, Molly," Divinity assured her. "It is just that she doesn't know how to help make things better, and she feels useless, so she stays away instead. Sometimes people ignore things so they don't seem so real. Your mom doesn't want to think that it could happen to you."

"But, Divinity, is there something WE can do to help?" asked Billy.

Divinity smiled at Billy, seeing the way he had changed, and how he now wanted to help other people when they were sad. "Yes, Billy, we can help," Divinity answered. "Little Beth needs to know she has friends she can talk to about this, because she has questions she needs answers to, and she doesn't want to ask her parents because she knows they are upset. She doesn't want to make them more sad."

"But how do we do that?" asked Brin. "We don't know her very well. Won't she think it's strange if we all go to see her?"

"No, Brin. She will see that you want to help by being her friend, and that will make her feel better," explained Divinity.

"But what if she dies?" sobbed Molly.

"I can see that you are very upset, Molly, but you must know that we all will die sometime, and it is nothing to be afraid of. It is a natural part of life. When Beth is able to talk about her fears, it will help her see things differently," said Divinity. "You can give her hope by showing her that you care."

The children were all very quiet for awhile, each lost in their own thoughts, and even a little bit afraid. None of them had ever known anyone who had actually died before, and they weren't sure they would know what to do or say to Beth.

Divinity understood all their thoughts, so she said "Just be yourselves and show you care, and the right words will be there. I am always with you, and I promised you I would help you to understand things that confuse you, and I will."

CHAPTER 7 LESSONS

Ask---When you need something that will help others, ask God to help, and good things will happen.

Denial---Sometimes when things happen that are uncomfortable to talk about, we just ignore the facts. This is called denial. We think if we don't think about it, it will go away, but not facing the truth never solves anything.

Desire to help another---When you truly care about people and their needs, a way will come to show you the right way to help. The desire to help comes from Love.

Make it real---When you focus your attention on something, whether it is "good" or "bad", it becomes more real to you. If it needs to be changed, it first has to be as real as you can make it so you can deal fully with it.

Offer to talk---When people are afraid of something, they may not know how to talk about it for fear of upsetting others. But to talk about things that are bothering you lightens your load because you can share it with someone who cares.

CHAPTER 8

Meeting Beth

The next day, Molly told her mother she wanted to go see Beth. "Oh Molly, her family is upset. I don't think that is a very good idea," said Mrs. Bennett.

"But Mom," Molly persisted, "Maybe Beth needs someone her own age to talk to and be her friend."

Mrs. Bennett could see Molly really had a desire to do something to help Beth. She still wasn't sure it was a good idea, but she told Molly she could go see Beth if she really wanted to. "But don't get in the way over there, Molly," cautioned Mrs. Bennett as Molly went out the door.

Brin and Billy were ready to go when she got to Brin's house. The boys weren't sure what they could do to help, but they knew Molly needed them to go along. After all, they knew somehow Divinity would be there, too. As they walked to Beth's house, they were very quiet. They were all wondering what to say. Out of nowhere, they all heard a voice say "Just be yourself and show you care," and they knew that Divinity was with them, even though they couldn't see her.

When they reached Beth's house, they put smiles on their faces and knocked on the door. Mrs. Parker came to the door, and was surprised to see three smiling children standing on her porch. No one had been smiling much at the Parker house recently, so she put a smile on her own face, and opened the door. "Hello, kids, what can I do for you?" she asked.

"Hello, Mrs. Parker," Molly began. "We heard Beth wasn't feeling well, so we came to visit with her, and see if she needs anything."

Mrs. Parker could see that the children really meant well, and she held back her tears. "Come in, kids, Come in," she said. "Beth is in her room. She is quite sick, but she will be happy to see you." Mrs. Parker led the way to Beth's room. She knocked on the door, and when Beth said to come in, her mother told her she had visitors.

"Really, Mom? Someone to see me?" she asked. Without another word, Molly, Brin and Billy came into her room, smiling at the sick girl in her bed.

"Hi Beth. Remember me? I'm Molly, and this is Brin and Billy. We heard you were sick, and thought you might, well, I mean, maybe you, um, well, we thought you might need some friends. Oh, maybe I didn't say that right. What I meant was...."

"It's okay, Molly--- I know what you mean. You're right! I do want some friends. It seems like since I got sick, I have been all alone. Nobody knows what to say to me. Everyone is uncomfortable around me, and I have been very lonely. Come in. I am glad you are here!" And Beth smiled back at the new friends in her room.

So the kids came in and sat down on Beth's bed, and chatted a little, and asked if there was anything they could do to help. "You're here, aren't you?" she asked, "and that's the most important thing!"

CHAPTER 8 LESSONS

Let go---Sometimes we don't know what the right thing to do is. We need to let go of our own ideas, and let others lead the way.

Be yourself---When in doubt as to how to approach a dilemma, just be yourself, and trust you will be shown the right way and given the right words to do your best.

Acceptance of the gift---In times of need, sometimes we isolate ourselves, feeling like we can handle the tough stuff alone. When someone cares enough to offer the gift of themselves, the best thing to do is to accept it. In this way, not only are you getting help that you may need, but in accepting help, you bless the giver. When a gift is offered, take it. The giver then feels better, too.

Do what you know is right---We all know right from wrong, because when we do the right thing, it feels good inside. Don't worry if you stumble along the way, because it isn't how you stumble, but that you offer to help another, and that is the right thing to do.

Support---When someone you know is in a difficult situation, just standing by them and letting them know you support their decisions makes it easier for them.

CHAPTER 9

Understanding

Beth was very happy that she had some new friends. She really HAD been alone since she got sick, and now things seemed much brighter. The kids didn't stay long, but they promised to return the next day. "Is there anything we can bring when we come tomorrow?" asked Brin cheerfully.

"Well, since you asked, I do love the summer flowers, and I can't see them from my bed. I would really like to have some flowers in my room, but I don't want anyone to go to any trouble," said Beth excitedly.

"Will do!" chimed the three children sitting on Beth's bed. "See you tomorrow!" and off they went.

Once outside, they couldn't help smiling real smiles. "She's really nice," said Billy.

"Yes," Brin added, "and it wasn't so hard to be with her, either."

"I have a feeling we are doing her some good," Molly thought out loud.

What they didn't know was how much Beth would help them, too!

The next afternoon, flowers in hand, they called on Beth again. Mrs. Parker opened the door to see three happy children, all with a bouquet of flowers in their hands. "Oh, Beth loves flowers!" exclaimed Mrs. Parker. "Why didn't I think of that?"

"You've been busy with Beth, Mrs. Parker," said Molly, "and we asked her what she wanted, so here we are. Can we see her now?"

"Of course, come on in, where are my manners?" said Mrs. Parker, and in they came.

Beth was sitting up in bed, awaiting her visitors. "Look at the pretty flowers, Mom! Do you have some vases to put them in?"

"Yes, of course dear," and she hurried off to find the vases. It felt good to Mrs. Parker to do something to help her daughter feel better. After the flowers were put around Beth's room, Beth thanked her mom, and Mrs. Parker left the children to play.

"I brought some cards" said Brin, "want to play Go Fish?" So the children spent the afternoon playing cards and laughing and being kids. It was the most fun Beth had had in a long time. All too soon, it was time to leave, so Brin gathered up his cards.

"Wait before you go, please," said Beth. "I just want to say I feel so much better because of you. I was starting to feel like nobody cared about me, and then you all showed up. It's funny, too, because the day you came over to see me, I was so sad, and I was wishing I had someone to talk to, and there you were! Three new friends. I don't understand. It's like I wished for you, and my wish came true. Has that ever happened to you?"

Molly, Brin and Billy started giggling and looked knowingly at each other. None of them was quite sure how to answer Beth. Molly went first. "Yes, Beth, I know just what you mean. When summer vacation started, Brin and I wished for a special adventure. We built a clubhouse in the woods, and, well, we got what we asked for!" Molly was giggling again because she didn't know how much to tell Beth.

Then Billy said, "I was new in town, and didn't have any friends either. I was lonely, and I wished for a friend, and I, uh, well, I MET Molly and Brin". And he started giggling, too.

Well, you can imagine how confused Beth was now! A magic clubhouse that makes wishes come true? No, it couldn't be. Those kids must be teasing her. Were they making fun of her because she was sick? Well, she supposed she would just wait and see.

CHAPTER 9 LESSONS

Don't be afraid to help---When you see someone is in need, just ask what you can do to help. When the question comes from your heart, it will be received well.

Face your fears---Once you do something you fear, it is no longer as scarey. The fear comes from not knowing outcomes. Once you just DO IT, you know the results, so the fear goes away.

Simple tasks---Sometimes in a situation that seems so large, such as illness or death, we don't know what to do, so we do nothing. If we think small and do simple things, it takes a part of the load off the sufferer.

Define---When something doesn't make sense, take it apart, piece by piece, and ask the right questions. When you do that, you will find the answers you seek.

CHAPTER 10

Beth Meets Divinity

True to their word, her new friends came by the next day. They weren't sure how they could explain Divinity to Beth, but they had faith that Divinity would show them the way. They went to Beth's house just knowing that they would find the right answers.

"Hi Molly and Brin and Billy!" said Beth when the children arrived. "I sure hope you can explain this clubhouse to me. I have been wondering about this all night!"

The children sat down, and Molly and Brin told Beth about how they built the clubhouse from just an idea. They were careful to explain the process, and how they had learned the lessons in creating their special place.

Then Billy told her how he had watched them having so much fun, and how mad he was about it. He explained he hadn't been very happy, but he didn't know why he was so mad that they were happy and he wasn't. He told her how he wanted to destroy the clubhouse and put an end to their happiness! "I started to wreck the clubhouse, and Brin caught me, and he was going to punch me in the nose!" said Billy.

"I can see why Brin would do that" agreed Beth, "but what stopped you?"

"Well," began Molly, "we have a special friend, and she showed up just in time."

"A special friend? I don't get it. How did she know Brin was going to punch Billy if she wasn't even there?" asked Beth.

"She is always with us, Beth," answered Brin, "and she is here right now. She helps us to understand things that confuse us. Do you want to meet her?"

Now Beth was REALLY confused. There were only four people in the room. What could they be up to? But she decided that she had to find out. "Yes, I want to meet her," she said bravely.

"Well then, close your eyes and she will be here," instructed Molly.

Beth had nothing to lose by playing along, so she closed her eyes, and hoped the kids weren't teasing her. "Hello, Beth," came the voice out of nowhere. Beth opened her eyes, and there was Divinity, fluttering over her bed! She was just as surprised as the other kids had been when they first saw Divinity!

"Is this a trick?" gasped Beth, not sure she was really seeing this beautiful being in her room.

"No, Beth, this is Divinity," explained Molly. "SHE is our special friend, and she told us to come and visit you. She helps us to know things we are confused about, and helps us by answering our questions. If you truly have a need to see her, she will be here for you."

"Yes, I have many questions," said Beth slowly. "Can you really help me, Divinity?"

Now Beth knew that she wasn't just seeing things, and she had heard Divinity speak, so she knew she was real, even if she didn't understand.

"Yes, Beth, I will help you to understand whatever you need to know. How can I help you?"

"Divinity, I am very sick. Am I going to die?" asked Beth in her bravest voice.

"Death comes to us all in our own time, my dear. We never know when it will happen, but it always does," explained Divinity gently. "When your time comes, you will know, and it will be okay. Dying is like being born into a different kind of life. Do you understand?"

"Kind of", Beth began, "but I am afraid. I don't want to leave my family, and my mom and dad will be sad," said Beth with tears in her eyes.

"We always fear things we don't know," said Divinity. "But I am here to help you understand. Ask me anything you want, and I will do my best to explain."

"Will it hurt?" was Beth's next question.

Divinity looked lovingly at Beth, and answered, "No Beth, it is like you just leave your body behind. There is no pain, and you will feel love and peace. You will go to another place, but you can still watch over your mom and dad, and they will know that you are no longer ill."

"Like an angel?" asked Beth, her eyes widening.

"Yes, JUST like an angel," replied Divinity. "And when it is time for your mom and dad to leave this life, they will be with you again. We never lose the ones we love."

"Will I be able to get out of my bed again, and go outside?" was Beth's next question.

"It is possible, because it is your wish," said Divinity. "Now that you have your new friends to help you focus on getting well, miracles can happen. I have been teaching them how to focus their attention on bringing about what it is they want, and with everybody doing their part, it just might work!"

"Oh, I hope so!" exclaimed Beth with a new hope in her heart. "Will you teach me, too?"

"Yes, Beth, that is why I am here. Since you believe in me, anything is possible. Just remember two things: One, have no expectations for a certain result, and Two, accept whatever happens with grace," explained Divinity.

"Okay," agreed Beth. "When can we start?"

"We already have, Beth. Just by your desire to see me, and your wish to be well again. But I think you've learned enough today. Spend time with your parents, and tomorrow we will be back." And with that, Divinity was gone!

Beth was tired but happy. She never would have believed what had just happened if she hadn't seen it for herself. But now, she not only had FOUR new friends, but new hope in her life. She said goodbye to Molly, Brin and Billy, and laid down to think about her wonderful experience.

CHAPTER 10 LESSONS

Second GUESS---When you think about things that you hear about, sometimes you don't believe what has been said, and you have thoughts that what you heard may not be true.

Be open to explanations---If something sounds too good to be true, try to be open minded and ask questions. Then wait for an explanation, and see if it makes more sense.

Faith---Faith is believing that even things that can't be seen can turn out to be true. Faith is Believing.

Decide---When you decide to make up your mind to be open to things that can't be seen, you learn new things and receive new opportunities to grow.

Proof---Proof happens when you see with your own eyes and hear with your own ears. Your experience of any event brings Faith in the experience to Proof of it's existence.

With no expectations, there can be no disappointment---When you ask for something to be given or to happen, let go of any expected results. Without expecting a certain result, you cannot be disappointed in the outcome.

Trust---To trust is to have faith that things will turn out for the best.

CHAPTER 11

Anything is Possible

Molly, Brin and Billy left Beth's house with mixed feelings. "You know, I just never thought much about what happens when you die," mused Billy out loud.

"Me neither," agreed Molly and Brin. They were quiet as they walked home.

"Do you suppose it's true?" wondered Molly aloud.

"What?" asked the boys together.

"That it's possible that Beth could get well," answered Molly.

"Well, Divinity said so," Brin started slowly, "and she has never been wrong before. I don't believe she would lie just to make Beth feel better, do you?"

"No!" replied Billy and Molly together.

"Then it MUST be true!" exclaimed Brin. "I wonder how we are supposed to help?"

"Well, Divinity showed us how with Billy's dad," Molly replied.

"Remember, we closed our eyes and wished for Billy's dad to find a job, and after awhile, when we thought about it every day, he got a job!"

"Divinity called that 'focusing out attention," said Billy in a knowing way. "I think wishes are different than focusing."

"Yes, I guess you're right," said Molly. "So we just focus our attention on Beth getting well, and she will!"

"But Molly," cautioned Brin, "remember what Divinity said about not expecting things to happen the way we think they should? I think that's important to remember."

"Yeah," said Billy. "I kept imagining Dad getting a job as a doctor, but he's working in the grocery store. It's a job, but not the one I wished for."

"Right!" Brin said. "There must be a certain way to do it, and we just have to believe that whatever is best for Beth will happen!"

"And always focus your attention with love," came the voice from nowhere.

"Aw, Divinity, we should've known you were here!" cried Molly. "You really ARE always with us, aren't you?"

"Yes, children, I promised I would be, and I always keep my promises!"

"Well then, HOW do we help Beth?" asked Brin.

"You are already helping her, even if you don't know it. You have made her your new friend, and no matter what happens, friendship is always a gift. You have given of yourself unselfishly, expecting nothing in return, and that is what love is. Always remember that when you give to another, whether it is a present or your presence, when you give it because you care, you have done a great thing."

"But we WANT to be her friend," said Molly. "It's not like it's a big deal."

"Aahhhh, but it IS a big deal to a very sick girl who was feeling all alone. Just your being her friend has given her hope, and with hope, all things are possible."

"But shouldn't we do MORE than just be her friend?" asked Billy. "What about that focus thing?"

"Well Billy, that focus thing can also be called prayer. Do you know what prayer is?" asked Divinity.

"Sure, it's saying thank you for your food before you eat," said Billy.

"Prayer is more than just being grateful," Divinity explained. "It IS focusing on what it is you wish to draw into your life, giving it the attention to draw it to you, and THEN being grateful for whatever way it is granted. Remember…no expectations," cautioned Divinity.

"But is there a way we can guarantee that Beth will get better if we focus on it?" pleaded Molly.

"No Molly, you just have to have faith that whatever is Beth's destiny will happen for her. You can never have a guarantee, but you have done so much just by being brave enough to offer her your friendship and give her hope. No one else has done that for her, so that makes the three of you very special kids!" said Divinity as she beamed with love for these three wonderful children.

"Okay then," said Molly, "We'll give it our best shot, won't we boys?"

"Yes we will," said Billy and Brin. "See you tomorrow, Molly!"

CHAPTER 11 LESSONS

Desire To help---Helping because we feel we HAVE to is different than having a desire to help because we WANT to. The first way is a duty, and the second way is giving of ourselves.

Focus attention with love---To focus attention as an observer is cold and clinical, but to focus attention with LOVE is to open your heart to another with a real desire to help.

Give of yourself---When you give of yourself, you are giving a real gift, not something artificial that could be given by just anyone for any reason.

CHAPTER 12

The Healing Begins

When the children went to visit with Beth the next day, they found her sitting in a chair in the living room. "Hello, Friends!" called Beth cheerfully as they came into the house.

"Wow, Beth!" exclaimed Brin with wonder in his voice, "You must be feeling better!"

"Oh, yes!" said Beth. "I had the most wonderful dream last night!"

"What was your dream?" asked Billy.

"I dreamed of the clubhouse!" replied Beth excitedly. "I dreamed I went there!"

"Wow!" said all three children, just as excited as Beth.

"I know I can't really go there, not yet," said Beth, "but I have something to give you to put in the clubhouse if you want."

"Sure, Beth, what is it?" asked Molly.

"Well, it's kind of silly," Beth began, "but it would mean a lot to me if you wanted to put it in the clubhouse. It is a picture my grandmother gave to me. It is a bluebird singing in a tree. It is singing because it is happy, and you said the clubhouse is called The Happy Place, so I thought it would fit. Do you want to put it in there?"

"Yes, Beth, that would be great," said Brin "If you really want to give it to us."

"I really do Brin," said Beth. "You have given me so much by being my friends, and I just want you to have it because it is special to me."

"Thanks Beth....we would love to have it," said Molly.

"Okay then, it's yours!" said Beth.

"NO, it's OURS," said Billy "because you are a part of our club now too, you know!"

Beth was so happy to hear that the kids wanted her to be a part of the club! "Well, what do you DO in your clubhouse?" asked Beth.

"We plan stuff we want to do," said Brin, "and we play in the woods, and swim in the pond. We take our lunch and eat it under the trees."

"Tell me more!" said Beth. "What is it like?"

"Well," began Molly, "it is a quiet place in the woods where it is peaceful, and easy to focus on the things we want to bring into our lives. There are animals all around, and butterflies and frogs and stuff. There are birds singing in the trees, too."

"Wow!" said Beth. "It sounds just wonderful. I want to go there someday."

"Well, Divinity said if we focus our attention on you getting well, it could happen," said Billy, "so let's try it!"

The kids all four closed their eyes and imagined that they were all four there. What a wonderful thought that was! It truly was a happy place!

"I feel like anything is possible!" said Beth. "When will you go there again and put our picture up?"

"I have an idea," said Brin, "let's go there now! Beth, you imagine that you are going with us. Just focus on going through the woods. Hear the birds singing in the trees, and see the squirrels playing tag in the woods, and the butterflies flying over the path."

"And the frogs in the pond!" said Billy, laughing.

"We haven't been there for a few days," said Molly. "Let's go hang the picture!"

CHAPTER 12 LESSONS

Dreams---Dreams are unconscious thoughts becoming real in your mind. It is where inspiration begins.

Appreciation---When you receive something from another person, showing that you appreciate it seals the gift and creates a bond.

Acceptance---When another person accepts your gift, it is like getting a gift back from them.

Quiet place to focus---It is easier to focus your thoughts when you are somewhere that is quiet and peaceful, and you feel safe and uninterrupted.

Creating a reality---To create something new in your life, first you have to think it in your mind, then believe it in your heart, and then it will happen. The hard part is to believe that it WILL happen, without any doubt.

CHAPTER 13

A New Surprise

Molly, Brin and Billy picked up the bluebird picture and thanked Beth again for the gift. They promised to come back in a day or so to see how she was doing. "Remember, Beth, if you get lonely or sad or anything, Divinity will come and visit you, even if we're not here. She said all you have to do is close your eyes and ask her to come, and she will be here for you. You ARE a member of the club now!" reminded Molly.

'Thanks for reminding me!" said Beth. "I will call on her and tell her about my dream. See you soon!"

The kids were excited to go to the clubhouse. It had been a few days since they were there, because they had been focusing on Beth and how they could help her. As they walked through the woods, they noticed that the flowers were in full bloom, and that reminded them of Beth, and how she loved flowers. It was as if she really WAS with them. This made them even happier than they already were.

When the kids reached the clubhouse, they noticed something

different. They weren't sure what it was, but they all felt it inside. Billy stopped before they got to the door, and asked, "Do you feel it?"

Molly and Brin nodded slowly, but nobody knew what it was. Looking around, everything seemed the same, but it 'felt' different. Instead of going into the clubhouse, Molly went to the window and pushed the curtain to one side and looked in. She gasped, and put her hand to her mouth!

"What is it, Molly?" whispered Brin urgently.

"Look for yourself!" Molly whispered back. Billy and Brin looked in the window and their mouths fell open!

"Who IS that?" whispered Billy.

"I don't know," replied Brin, "I can't see his face."

"Well, we'd better find out," said Molly, and the three kids went through the doorway. What they saw was a boy about their age, curled up in a blanket---their DOOR---on the ground, fast asleep. "What should we DO?" Molly whispered again.

"We better wake him up and see what he's doing in our clubhouse!" decided Brin.

"Hey, Kid!" said Billy in a loud voice, "wake up!"

The boy on the ground awoke with a start. He looked around like he didn't know where he was at first, and then he saw the kids standing around him, staring. He pulled the blanket close around him and looked scared. The kids could see that he had been crying, and they weren't so mad anymore.

"Who are you?" asked Brin gruffly.

"Who are YOU?" asked the boy.

"This is our clubhouse," said Billy. "What are you doing here anyway? You're trespassing!"

"I'm sorry," said the boy. "I didn't know anyone lived here."

"We don't LIVE here," explained Molly, "we PLAY here. What are you doing in our clubhouse?"

"I don't have anywhere else to go," said the boy, "and I thought maybe I could live here until I figure something out."

The kids looked at each other in disbelief. They weren't quite sure what to say to this boy. "What's your name?" asked Molly in a nicer tone. She didn't want to scare the boy anymore than he already was.

"I'm Timmy."

"Why are you here?" asked Brin.

"I told you…I have nowhere to go," said Timmy.

"Where are your parents?" Molly asked.

Then Timmy really began to cry. "I'm sorry, I didn't know this was your clubhouse. I'll leave now."

"Wait!" said Billy, "Where are your parents?"

Timmy looked at the kids with big sad eyes. "My mom is at home in town, I guess, and my dad is gone. I don't know where he is. He just left us, and it's all my fault," and he started to cry again.

Well, the kids didn't know what to do or say. But if ever there was a time for Divinity to be there to help, this was the time! "You stay here for a minute, Timmy," Brin instructed, "We need to have a club meeting----outside!" and Molly and Billy followed him out the door.

"What should we DO?" asked Billy.

"We can't just have Divinity come here so Timmy gets all scared of her. He wouldn't understand!" was Molly's answer.

"Well, he can't stay HERE!" said Brin.

"His mother must be worried if she doesn't know where he is," Molly insisted.

"We better go talk to him," Brin decided, so they all went back into the clubhouse to deal with this new development.

CHAPTER 13 LESSONS

Divinity is always with you---Once you become aware that you always have a special friend with you, you know you're never alone.

Awareness---When you notice that things 'feel' different, you are being aware of changes.

Intuition---Intuition is when you 'feel' something has changed, but you can't see it, you just 'know' it inside.

Unexpected development---Sometimes when things are going along smoothly, a new development comes into play that throws you off course.

Take matters in your hands---When you have an unexpected development, sometimes you have to think fast and do what you have to to figure it out.

CHAPTER 14

Timmy's Sadness

The kids came back into the clubhouse to talk to Timmy and see just what was going on. "Okay, Timmy," Brin began, "this is our clubhouse, and you are in it, so you owe us an explanation, don't you think?"

"You're right, I guess, but I can just leave. Nobody wants me around here anyway, so I should just go," replied Timmy sadly. "Sorry about the blanket, but I was kind of cold last night."

"Hold on, you're not going anywhere!" said Billy.

"You SLEPT here last night?" asked Molly in disbelief.

"Yes," said Timmy.

"Your mother must be worried SICK!" said Molly.

"No, she's better off without me," Timmy replied.

"What are you talking about?" asked Molly.

"My dad left yesterday. I heard him yelling at my mom. I couldn't hear everything they said, but I heard my name several times. I just know it's my fault that he left, and if I go away, maybe he'll come back, and my mom will quit crying," explained Timmy sadly.

Well, this was more than the kids could handle by themselves, but how were they supposed to deal with Timmy when they called on Divinity? What a dilemma! They couldn't let Timmy leave, and they didn't know how to explain Divinity, even thought they knew she could fix this problem.

"Okay, Timmy, we'll help you, but you have to trust us," offered Molly. "My name is Molly, and this is Brin and Billy. First of all, we need to get you back home. Your mom is probably worrying like crazy. Do you trust us?"

"Do I have a choice?" asked Timmy slowly.

"You always have a choice, Timmy," said Billy. "But if your dad really left, then you are the man of the house, and you have to take care of your mom, and you're not doing that by being here!"

"My dad IS gone," Timmy replied. "He said something about a divorce, and took his suitcase."

"Well then, let's get you home so your mom isn't alone," said Molly in her practical voice.

"But…." started Timmy…..

"No buts!" said Brin. "Molly said we will help you with this, but you have to trust us. Do you?"

"Well, I don't know what else to do," sighed Timmy, "and I AM pretty hungry, and I don't have any money, so I guess I will have to trust you. Do you PROMISE you will help me if I go back home?"

"Yes," said all three kids.

"But HOW can you help me?" Timmy wondered suspiciously.

"Molly has a plan," said Brin. He didn't know what else to say because he had no idea what they were going to do, but he had to sound convincing to Timmy to get him to go home so his mom would quit worrying. Brin gave Molly a look that said "you'd better have a plan!"

"Okay, I trust you," Timmy sighed, "let's go."

So they all followed Timmy through the woods and into town, wondering silently what they would do next.

CHAPTER 14 LESSONS

Gather Facts---When something comes up that you don't know how to deal with, first gather the facts so you can make an informed decision.

Misplaced responsibility---When things go wrong with our parents' lives, sometimes we think it is our fault, and we blame ourselves, but this is usually not the case.

How to help?---Sometimes HOW you can help someone is not clear right away, so you need time after you gather the facts to make sure the decision IS clear.

You always have a choice---There are many choices when it comes to making a decision. Weigh the facts carefully and decide which choice you think is best. If it doesn't work, make a different choice until you find the right one.

Stick together---If there is more than one person making choices, be sure to trust each other enough to stick together and work on it as a team.

CHAPTER 15

The Plan

"Okay, here's my house," announced Timmy. "Now what do we do?"

The children could sense that Timmy had given them his full trust, and felt very responsible to be his support. They HAD promised a plan, so it was up to them to make the next move.

"Well, Timmy," Molly began, when all at once the door of Timmy's house burst open and his mother cried "Timmy! Where have you BEEN? I have been so worried about you! I have the police out looking for you! Oh, my son!" and she started to cry.

"It's okay, Mom," sniffled Timmy. "I was going to run away, but these kids found me and told me I needed to come home so you wouldn't worry."

Mrs. Miller looked at the children with gratitude in her eyes. "Thank you children! Thank you very much!"

"It's okay," said Brin. "We found him in our clubhouse, and we want to be his friends. Is it okay if we come back tomorrow to play?"

Mrs. Miller looked at the three children, and realized that Timmy would need some good friends. She knew he was upset that his father had left, and sometimes kids his own age might be more helpful to him than she could be. "Yes, of course you may," she said. "We will see you in the morning."

So Molly, Brin and Billy said goodbye to Timmy and went over to Molly's house to think up a plan. "I thought you HAD a plan, Molly," accused Brin. "We trusted you!"

"My plan was to get Timmy home to his mother, and figure out how to help him later," Molly said in her own defense.

"Well then, we'd better come up with a plan," said Billy.

"I think we should take Timmy back to the clubhouse tomorrow," said Molly. "I just KNOW Divinity can help. It's just how do we explain her to Timmy so he will understand?"

"Well, you explained her to ME," said Billy, "and to Beth. Why wouldn't Timmy understand?"

"He seems like kind of a scaredy-cat," explained Molly. "He is so upset about his dad."

"Yeah," said Brin, "but Divinity has never failed us before! Let's go to the clubhouse and see what she has to say!"

So the children went quickly back to the clubhouse, sat down, closed their eyes, and called for Divinity to help them. In the twinkling of an eye she appeared.

"What can I do for you kids?" asked Divinity "What do you need to know today?"

"Oh Divinity, I am so glad you are here!" cried Molly "We have a BIG problem….."

"Yes, I know," replied Divinity. "You don't know what to do to help Timmy."

The kids just stared at her. "But how did you know that?" asked Billy.

Divinity just smiled, but she seemed a little sad. "I have told you before, I am always with you, especially at times when you need me the most. You can call on me ANY time, and I will be there. Do you believe me?"

"Oh yes!" the children replied together.

"I am sorry we doubted you, Divinity," said Brin slowly. "It's just that we were so surprised when we found Timmy, we were confused."

"And THAT is when you need me most," stated Divinity. "Please never forget that when you ask me to be there for you, even when you are the most confused, I can help you."

The children felt a little foolish for forgetting that Divinity had made them a promise, and they had forgotten that she really WAS always there for them. No problem could ever be too big or too small to take to Divinity, and they felt ashamed. Divinity picked up on their feelings right away. "You don't need to feel bad, children," she said lovingly. "Sometimes it takes a hard lesson to remember what I have told you. Because you feel ashamed, you will always remember this lesson. Feeling ashamed of your actions means you have grown beyond the choice you made, and chances are you will never make the same choice because you know you made the wrong one. It is in this way that we learn our lessons, and remember them. Now, let's focus on Timmy. I think he might surprise you."

"Okay Divinity, what's the plan?" asked Molly.

"Well, if you can bring Timmy to the clubhouse tomorrow, and find a way to introduce him to me, I will be there to help. Your job is to think about how you will do that," and with that, she was gone.

So the children made a plan to go see Timmy the next day, bring him to the clubhouse, and SOMEHOW make him feel comfortable with the idea of a fairylike being who could talk to him and help him with his sadness.

CHAPTER 15 LESSONS

Responsibility---When you give someone your word, you must follow through and keep it. In this way, trust is established, and people will be more likely to listen to you.

First things first---Sometimes in order to do a certain thing, there are other things that need to be done to prepare the way. Never skip over details that will lay a strong foundation for what you are about to do. You have to start at the beginning.

When in doubt, ask for help---There is nothing wrong with asking for help. In times of doubt, or need, it not a sign of weakness that we are showing, but humility. When we ask humbly for guidance, we receive it more fully.

Always there---The most important principle we can ever know is we are never alone. Our guidance is always with us, because it is WITHIN us. All we have to do is be humble, and ask for what we need.

Never deny the Light of Truth---Truth has always been with us, and always will be. You can forget it, or ignore it, but it is a fact that it is always there, just for the asking.

Lessons---When we forget that the truth is always there, and make poor choices, we feel ashamed. But shame is just a tool to remember that we made a bad choice, so we will always remember never to do the same thing again. Life is full of lessons, and how we grow from them makes us who we are.

CHAPTER 16

Timmy's Surprise

The next day, the kids went to Timmy's house and told Mrs. Miller where they were going. They promised to bring Timmy back before supper. As they walked through the woods, Brin had to ask Timmy a question. "Timmy, weren't you afraid to run away from home? I mean, where did you think you could go that nobody could find you?"

"Well, Brin, the truth is, I was so upset I just didn't think about that. I just needed to get away, so I took off. Then I found your clubhouse, and it just felt like that was the place I had to be. It was kind of scary to be alone, and I could hear sounds all around me, and I got even more scared, but something happened, and I knew it was going to be okay."

"What happened?" Molly interrupted with interest.

"Oh, I just felt peaceful, and fell asleep," said Timmy, kind of evasively. "I guess I was just tired from being so upset about my dad."

"Oh," said Molly. She knew that Timmy wasn't telling her the whole truth, but she thought maybe in time he would trust them enough to tell them the rest of the story. It didn't matter right now anyway, because she still hadn't thought of how to introduce Divinity to him.

They reached the clubhouse, and Timmy said, "I want to fix the door for you. I tore it down, and I noticed it was ripped, so I brought Mom's sewing needle and thread so I can fix it better than it was before, to thank you for being so nice to me. How'd it get ripped, anyway?"

Molly, Brin and Billy started laughing, and while he was fixing the door, they told Timmy the story about how they came up with the idea for the clubhouse, and how they built it. Then they told him the part about Billy wanting to wreck it, and how he tore the blanket apart right before Brin was going to punch him in the nose. Timmy was laughing at the thought if it, because he couldn't imagine his three new friends ever being mad at each other! "So, why didn't you punch him?" asked Timmy, laughing out loud.

"Something stopped me," answered Brin. "If you just come into the clubhouse, we will tell you how we knew that fighting wasn't the best choice."

"Okay," said Timmy. "I'm finished with my repairs. Let's hang the door back up." And so they did.

Once inside the clubhouse, Molly asked everyone to sit down. She still wasn't sure how Timmy would respond to meeting Divinity, but she had faith that it would all work out. "Timmy, we are going to close our eyes for a minute, and center ourselves."

"What is 'center ourselves'?" inquired the new boy.

"That means we just relax for a minute, and get our thoughts together. We have something to share with you that is VERY important!" Said Molly, feeling very important herself.

"Okay, I can do that," agreed Timmy. So they all closed their eyes, and in a moment, Divinity was there, sitting quietly on the picture of the bluebird that was hanging on the wall in front of Timmy.

"Okay, now open your eyes, Timmy. What do you see?" asked Molly.

Timmy opened his eyes, and looked right at Divinity. He just smiled. He didn't seem upset at all!!

"Can you see her?" asked Timmy of the kids.

The children were shocked! They thought for sure this scared little boy would have jumped up and run out of the clubhouse when he saw Divinity, but here he was, calmly smiling at her as if he already knew her!

"Can YOU?" asked Brin, quite surprised.

"Of course!" replied Timmy. "She lives here. I saw her the other night when I was trying to fall asleep. I was so scared, and all of a sudden, I saw her here with me, and I felt peaceful, like everything would be okay, so I fell asleep. I didn't think anyone would believe me, so I didn't tell you that part. Isn't she beautiful?"

Well, you can imagine their surprise that Timmy had already met Divinity! Even Divinity hadn't told them THAT part!

"Have you talked to her then?" questioned Billy.

"TALKED to her?" asked Timmy, taken by surprise.

"Yes, her name is Divinity, and she is here to help us when we are confused or sad or lonely. She says she is always here for us, and will answer all our questions if we just call on her and ask," replied Brin.

"Really?!" exclaimed Timmy. "I just thought she was my imagination, and that her peacefulness and beauty made me feel safe! I didn't know she could TALK!"

"That's because you didn't ASK," said Divinity. "When you first saw me, you only needed to be comforted, and feel like you were not alone, so I appeared to you for that reason."

NOW Timmy was surprised!

CHAPTER 16 LESSONS

You can't run from your feelings---No matter what kind of feelings we have, we can't run away from them. The best thing to do is to find a way to face them.

Trust your feelings--Your feelings are inside of you for a reason. You must learn to listen to them, and trust that they are right.

Time will tell---In time, everything will come to be explained, and you will understand why things happen the way they do.

Make amends---If you have done something you realize is wrong, it is important to apologize and make up for what you have done.

There are many ways to tell the truth---Sometimes we don't know exactly how to tell the truth, but do your best to say it in the kindest way possible.

Honesty---To be a good person, honesty is a very important quality. We must always be honest with ourselves and others.

There's more than meets the eye---Sometimes we are not aware of everything around us. It takes a great awareness to see everything in our path.

CHAPTER 17

Acceptance

"I thought I was just imagining you because I was tired and upset!" exclaimed Timmy.

"And that is all you needed then, Timmy," explained Divinity. "I am here to help you. Do you have any questions for me?"

"Yes…." said Timmy slowly, "I need to know why my dad doesn't love me anymore, and why he left. I don't know what I did wrong."

Tears were again welling up in Timmy's eyes as he remembered his hurt feelings. He didn't want to start crying again, but he just HAD to know.

"Your dad DOES love you Timmy. He loves you very much," said Divinity in her gentlest voice. "The reason he left has nothing to do with you."

"But I heard him saying my name when he was talking to my mom," sniffled Timmy. "I must have done something to make him leave."

"Timmy," Divinity began, "sometimes when people are married, there are problems that they can't seem to work through. This is very frustrating for the people involved, including the children. When this happens, sometimes the man and his wife have to take a break from their problems. It gives them time to think about how or if they can fix what is wrong."

"But maybe I'm the problem," said Timmy slowly, hoping he might be wrong.

"No, Timmy, you are not the problem. I happen to know that your mom and dad love you very much, and they want what is best for you, that's all," explained Divinity.

"But I don't think it's best for Dad to go away!" answered Timmy. "I need him, and I love him!"

"What you think is best, and what your parents think is best are not always the same thing. Only your parents know how they need to handle this problem, and you have to know that they will make the right decision for all of you," said Divinity.

"Will my dad come back?" asked Timmy hopefully.

"You will see him often, Timmy. You have to believe that this has nothing to do with you, and you did nothing wrong. Your parents just need time to figure things out. Can you understand that?" asked Divinity.

"Yes, I guess so," said Timmy slowly, "but I MISS him."

"And you will miss him for awhile, but you have to trust your parents and know they do love you," said Divinity. "When you truly love someone, you accept them for who they are, and honor their decisions, even though you may not agree with what they decide."

"Why won't he come home NOW?" asked Timmy.

"Your mom and dad need to sort things out. It is important that you allow them time, and have patience," Divinity explained. "Your dad will always be your dad, you know! Nothing can change that."

"But things won't be the same without him," moaned Timmy, really feeling the changes he would have to go through.

"No, life is full of change, Timmy. As you grow up, you will find that the one thing you can always count on is change," said Divinity. "Some changes are for the good, and sometimes it doesn't seem to be so good, but in the end, it all works out. You will find that everything happens for a reason."

"And we will be here for you to talk to!" encouraged Molly. "We learned from Divinity that when you have a problem that seems so big you can't handle it, friends can share your problems, and they don't seem so big anymore."

"Yeah, that's what friends do for each other Timmy," said Billy in a knowing voice. "I know, because Molly and Brin sure helped me when I was going through a hard time."

"And look at Beth," Brin added. "We help her by giving her hope, and she is teaching us that even when bad things happen, you can still be strong."

"Who's Beth?" asked Timmy, and for a moment he stopped thinking of his own problem.

"She is a girl we know who is very sick," explained Molly. "We were afraid to talk to her, because we didn't know what to say. But Divinity said it doesn't matter WHAT we say, only that we be ourselves and be her friend so she has someone to share her thoughts with."

"Can I meet her sometime?" asked Timmy. "Maybe I can help her, too!"

"That's very kind of you, Timmy. And meeting Beth will show you that although you have problems, some people have problems even bigger than yours," said Divinity.

"Is she very sick?" Timmy wanted to know.

"Yes, she is," said Molly sadly. "The doctors don't know if she will get better or not."

"Oh, that's terrible!" said Timmy. "I guess my problem isn't as awful as it seems. At least I have my mom and dad, and I know things will get better."

"See, Timmy, just hearing about Beth has helped you understand that life isn't always as bad as it seems," said Divinity.

"We'll go see her tomorrow," said Molly. "I miss her, and it's only been a few days since we saw her. She gave us that bluebird picture the day we met you!"

"Okay! I can hardly wait to meet her!" said Timmy.

CHAPTER 17 LESSONS

Blame---When things go wrong in our lives, we tend to blame ourselves. This is not always the case. We must look at the whole picture to find the truth.

Step back---When problems are hard to understand, we need to step away from them and see them from a different point of view.

Decisions---We make decisions everyday. People don't always agree with the decisions we make, nor do we agree with theirs. We all do what we think is best.

Patience---If we just have patience, we see that things work out the way they're supposed to, in their own time. We can't force things to happen.

Change---Life is full of changes. We have to accept change in our life, and do the best with what we have.

Everything happens for a reason---We may not understand why things happen, but we have faith that there is a reason for everything that does.

Bonding---When we share feelings with others, it creates a bond of trust, and we then feel that we are not alone.

Help others---When we see that someone needs our help, and we willing give them what they need, it takes our mind off our own problems, if only for awhile, and we see others have bigger problems than we do.

CHAPTER 18

Timmy Meets Beth

The next day, the children went to Timmy's house and asked Mrs. Miller if Timmy could come with them to Beth's house. "Isn't that the Parker's daughter that is so sick?" asked Mrs. Miller with concern.

"Yes, m'am," replied Molly. "She is our new friend, and we want Timmy to meet her."

"Are you sure it's such a good idea to be around such a sick child?" worried Mrs. Miller.

"Oh yes!" Brin assured her. "What Beth has is not catchy, and we make her happy when we go see her. It's okay!"

"Well, all right then," said Mrs. Miller. "Just don't get in the way!"

The kids smiled knowingly at each other, remembering how Molly's mother had said the same thing. "We won't," the children said together as they went happily out the door.

"What is Beth like?" asked Timmy. "I never met anyone who is really sick."

"We hadn't either, Timmy," said Molly "but Divinity told us just to be ourselves, so that is what we do, and it is easy to be with her. She's really nice."

"And brave!" added Brin.

Soon they were all at Beth's house, and knocked on the door. Mr. Parker answered the door, looking concerned.

"Is something wrong, Mr. Parker?" asked Billy.

"No, not really," replied Beth's father. "Beth and her mother are just having a talk about what is best for Beth."

"Well, can we see her, or is this a bad time?" asked Molly carefully. She wondered what could be going on.

"Let me check with her mother," answered Mr. Parker. "I will be right back."

The children looked at each other, and wondered what the problem was. Timmy looked the most confused. "Maybe we should leave…. maybe it's not the best day to meet Beth," wondered Timmy out loud. "Maybe we should just go now."

"No Timmy, just because we don't have all the facts doesn't mean we should run away like a baby," said Billy, before he realized what he had just said.

Timmy looked at Billy sadly, knowing that that is just what he had done when his dad left.

"I'm sorry, Timmy!" said Billy quickly. "I didn't mean YOU are a baby!"

'Words carelessly spoken can cause hurt feelings," came Divinity's voice.

"I know I acted like a baby, Billy," said Timmy carefully. "But now I know better than to run away from my problems, and I should have thought about that before I wanted to run away---you're right---thanks!" and Timmy smiled a big smile at Billy to let him know he really was okay.

"Sure," said Billy, looking down at his shoes. "I just didn't think before I said that. I really am sorry."

"Sometimes words must be spoken out loud in order to clarify a thought," said Divinity. The kids hadn't called on her, but she could feel that they needed her, so she appeared on the porch. "Sometimes we have to face our fears more than once to break the pattern of our habits. Some things are very hard to change."

"Like my dad's anger," said Billy, his face lighting up. "It took some time, but after awhile, he stopped taking out his frustrations by being mean to me!"

"That is correct, Billy. I am glad you understand," Divinity smiled. "Just remember, some things take time." And with that, she was gone.

Mr. Parker reappeared at the front door. "My wife thinks it would be okay for you to see Beth for a little while now. Please show yourselves to her room."

Not knowing what was going on made the children a little bit nervous, but they knew they had to face their fears and make sure Beth was okay. When they got to Beth's room, they could see she had been crying, and instead of trying to look brave, they all went and sat on her bed, and waited for her to tell them what was wrong.

"I'm so glad you're all here," said Beth. Then she noticed Timmy. "Oh, I look a mess! Who are you?"

"I'm Timmy. I wanted to meet you and be your friend. I just joined the club," said Timmy slowly.

"Oh," smiled Beth, "I'm glad to meet you! I need all the friends I can get right now."

"But what's wrong, Beth?" asked Molly. She couldn't stand wondering anymore why her friend looked so sad.

"My parents want to send me away," replied Beth. "They say it is a really nice hospital, where the doctors know all about my disease, and it will be best for me to go there, but I don't want to leave!" All this came tumbling out so fast that the children didn't quite know what to say.

"Please help me!" begged Beth.

CHAPTER 18 LESSONS

Protection----When we don't have all the facts about a situation, we want to protect the ones we love from the things we fear---the unknown.

Second Guess---Without all the facts, it is easy to change your mind and decide that MAYBE some other plan of action is better.

Get the facts---Until we understand what all the facts are, we shouldn't make any decision

Reacting---When we react to a situation sometimes we say things without thinking how it will affect others. Words carelessly spoken can hurt other people's feelings. Try to think before you speak.

Admit---Always admit when you are wrong, so you will remember next time to respond in a different way.

Breaking old habits---Our actions are a result of our conditioning. We all have good and bad habits that we need to look at. If it is a bad habit that we want to change, sometimes we have to repeat the lesson more than once to get it right.

CHAPTER 19

A Decision is Made

The children all sat in silence for a few minutes, getting their thoughts together. So many things were running through their minds. What was the best thing to do? What was the right thing to say? Timmy spoke up first. "I know I am new at this, but wouldn't this be a good time to talk to Divinity?" he asked "I mean, she DID promise to help us, and this is a pretty big problem."

"You're right, Timmy," said Brin, proud of the way this boy who used to be such a scaredy-cat was taking charge.

"Well, let's all close our eyes, and focus on Divinity then, and see what she has to say," said Molly, taking over quickly. And so they did.

In the twinkling of an eye, Divinity was there with the five children. "Why are you all looking so concerned?" she asked.

"My parents want me to go away," sniffled Beth "and I don't want to leave my new friends!"

"Maybe you haven't looked at all the facts yet," replied Divinity. "Can we take this one step at a time, and figure out what is best?"

"Yes," said the children all together. "But how do we do that?" asked Timmy.

"Go to the source for the answers---ask Beth's mom to come in here so you can all ask the questions you need to know the answers to. Then it will be easier to help Beth make a decision, for whatever happens is her choice. I will wait until you're finished talking," explained Divinity, and with that, she was gone.

"Good idea!" exclaimed Timmy knowingly. "Getting all the facts is important before you decide to do something!" He looked knowingly at the other kids, because now that he knew he wasn't the cause of his parent's problems, it was easier for him to deal with the fact that his dad was gone.

So Beth called Mrs. Parker into the room. "Mom, will you come here, please? We have some questions to ask you."

When Beth's mom came into the room, she saw five very thoughtful children all sitting on Beth's bed, so she sat down in the rocking chair next to the bed. "Well, what is it that you want to ask me?" said Mrs. Parker.

"Why do you want me to go away?" asked Beth directly.

"We don't want you to 'go away'," began Mrs. Parker. "It's just that this hospital is too far to drive to everyday, and the doctors need to have you there to observe you when they do the tests to see how your health is."

"Will you be with me?" asked Beth.

"Oh yes, honey!" replied Mrs. Parker, surprised that she hadn't thought of how Beth was thinking all of this would come about. "I will get a hotel room close by, and see you every day! You will never be alone!"

Beth felt better knowing that! She didn't want to be alone.

"What kind of a place is this?" asked Molly, thinking of big machines, and needles, and mean nurses.

"Well, it's a children's hospital," Mrs. Parker said. "And every patient is under 16 years of age, and there are activities with the other children when the doctors aren't running tests, and they have games and movies, and even a park right in the middle of the hospital ground!"

"Wow!" said Billy enthusiastically, "that sounds like a vacation!"

"That's a good way to look at it Billy," said Beth's mom, "only it's not just a fun place to go, but it will help us get the answers that we need for Beth, so it is even better!"

"But when will Beth come home?" asked Timmy.

"We have to wait for the doctors answers before we know that," replied Mrs Parker, "but Mr. Parker and I think this is the best way to help our daughter. What do you think, Beth?"

Beth thought for a few minutes, and then replied "Well, Mom, if you really believe this is the best thing to do, I will go. But I want to do one thing first."

"What's that?" asked Mrs. Parker, surprised at Beth's change of mind.

"I want to go to the clubhouse first, so I can see it in my mind when I am away. It will make it easier for me if I really know what it is like."

"But Beth! How will you get there?" asked her mother. "You can't walk that far, and we can't drive you there. Are you sure this is what you want to do?"

"Yes, Mom! If we find a way to do it, will you let me go?" pleaded Beth.

Mrs. Parker could see how much it meant to Beth to see the clubhouse, and she didn't want her to change her mind, so she agreed. "But if you do find a way, you must check with me first so I know it's safe, and not be gone too long," she said.

"I will, Mother!" laughed Beth excitedly. "Now we just have to figure out a way to get there!"

So, Mrs. Parker left the children to make their plans, wondering if there really was a way to make it work.

CHAPTER 19 LESSONS

Get the facts---To make a decision, you must gather together all the facts.

Go to the source---To find the facts, never rely on what others tell you. Go to the person who has the facts, and ask them directly.

Pros and Cons---Some facts may weigh in favor of a certain decision, and other facts may weigh against it. Make a list, and see how the facts appear on paper.

Compromise---If we want to make things happen, sometimes we have to give in to what someone else wants, too, and do one thing to get another. This is compromise.

Where there's a Will, there's a way---If you want something bad enough, and you explore all your resources, and use your WILL to help focus and create that which you want, you will find a way to accomplish it.

CHAPTER 20

The Clubhouse

The children were very excited about having permission to bring Beth to the clubhouse! Now they just had to figure out HOW to get her there.

"I know it will be hard for me to go all the way to the clubhouse," Beth began, "but if we all think hard, I just KNOW it can happen," she said meaningfully. "What is the first step?"

"Well," said Billy slowly, "let's all remember what Divinity has taught us. First we have to close our eyes and 'imagine' you there. Then we look back at how we got you to the clubhouse, and 'see' the steps it took to get you there."

"Okay," said Beth, "let's do that first."

So the children all closed their eyes and imagined their first time all together in the clubhouse. They thought of how much fun it would be, and how important it was for Beth to be there, so if she got lonely for her new friends, she could just close her eyes and pretend she was there.

"I see it!" cried Brin excitedly. "We'll put Beth in my wagon, with lots of pillows, and PULL her to the clubhouse!"

"Oh Brin! That's a GREAT idea!" exclaimed Molly, giggling at the thought of it.

"Well, what are we waiting for?" asked Billy, and all of them hugged Beth goodbye as they went to get the wagon ready. It didn't take long to turn the wagon into a chariot fit for a princess, and they were back at Beth's house in no time.

Beth had explained the plan to her parents, and even though they were a little worried about it, they could see how much it meant to their daughter, and they knew it would make her accept her hospital stay better, so they agreed. When Molly, Brin, Billy and Timmy got back to Beth's house, she was ready to go. Her father carried her to the wagon, and carefully placed her frail body on the pillows. The look of joy on her face almost made him cry. "You be back soon, you hear?" he said to the children.

"We will! Thank you Mr. Parker," and off they went.

You might think it was hard pulling the wagon filled with pillows and a small girl through a path in the woods, but the kids took turns and it wasn't hard at all. Along the path, they pointed out all the things that before they had only been able to tell Beth about. She was delighted to hear the catbirds, and see the squirrels, and soon she could even hear the frogs splashing in the pond.

"We're almost there, aren't we?" squealed Beth, happier than she had been in a long time.

"Yes, Beth, it's jut around the corner," replied Brin.

And there it was! The clubhouse that had started out as just an idea in the minds of two children, that had been a source of anger for Billy, and a safe place for Timmy. And who do you suppose was there waiting for them, but Divinity, just as happy as she could be!

"Well done, Children! You DID it! You were able to focus on a plan, and make it work! I am so proud of all of you," said Divinity. "Now let's bring Beth inside."

The children pushed the wagon inside, and Beth saw the bluebird picture hanging on the wall, the pretty curtain that the kids had peeked through when they found Timmy, and the patched up blanket they used for a door.

"It's like all the stories you have told me about this place are real now," said Beth. "I am so happy to really be here with all my new friends."

"And we are happy you were brave enough to come to see it!" said Molly with a small tear of happiness in her eye. "Mom packed us a special lunch in honor of Beth's arrival. Anyone want to eat?"

So the children ate their lunch in between telling each other new ideas for things they could do with the rest of their summer, and how they would keep a journal of all their adventures to share with Beth when she came home.

"We will focus on you every time we come here, Beth, so you will feel our energy with you, and get stronger," said Billy.

"And so you won't be lonely," added Timmy.

"And you can imagine all the fun we'll have together when you get home!" said Molly.

Brin looked thoughtfully at the happy group of children and Divinity, and said "I think I was right when I named the clubhouse "The Happy Place." I can't imagine a better name for it!"

Divinity smiled at the children and said, "It is all as it should be."

Printed in the United States
By Bookmasters